I CAN

DO WHAT THE BIBLE SAYS I CAN DO

JAKE & KEITH PROVANCE

WORD & SPIRIT
PUBLISHING

I CAN DO What the Bible Says I Can Do
ISBN: 978-1-936314-09-6
Copyright © 2019 by Word and Spirit Publishing

Published by Word and Spirit Publishing
P.O. Box 701403
Tulsa, Oklahoma 74170

Contents

Introduction

Most Christians live far below the level of fulfillment, joy, and quality of life that God desires for them. But that is not what God intended! It is essential for us to come to the realization that, through our relationship with Christ and by the power of God's Word, *we can do all things.* Anything He has told us to do, He provides along with the directive, the grace, empowerment, equipment, and help necessary to do it!

God sent His very own Spirit to dwell within us to empower, comfort, and guide us into the life He had always planned for us to have. We have the same Spirit that raised Christ from the dead living in us! The Christian condition is not a life of survival, barely making it through day by day. We are called to live a life of Faith, aggressively advancing under fire towards our God given destiny, with God's Word as the anchor for our souls, utilizing the gifts afforded to us as God's children, and depending on the Holy Spirit leadings and empowerments!

God never promised that the life of a believer would be one without challenges. He did promise the power and companionship to face these challenges head on—and to triumph over them. We are called, equipped, and supernaturally empowered to change our lives—and have a powerful impact on the lives of others.

We are sons and daughters of the Almighty God; we are not to look for pity and act like victims in our own lives. When the storm winds blow, a greater intimacy with our Father God will be forged as we trust in and rely on Him. When we find ourselves in the fiery crucible of crisis, we can be confident knowing that our faith is going to be tested, strengthened, and purified as we esteem the Word of God higher than life's greatest challenges. There is nothing this life can throw at us that we can't overcome! We are called to rise above life's difficulties with an unshakeable faith in God. A faith that comes from an uncompromising conviction in the never-failing, life-empowering, bondage-breaking, life-giving, and faith-producing nature of the Word of God. God's words are *alive,* and His commands and encouragements carry with them immeasurable power. It's time to tap into this power and elevate your perception, ability, and quality of life to the level God destined for you.

I encourage you to read on and let God heal your past, empower your present, and clarify your future. **It is time to do what the Bible says you can do.**

I Can Transform My Life

You have the power to transform your life completely. Do you want to go from victim to victor, from a failure to a success, from fearful to peaceful? You can go from depressed to joyful, from insecure to confident, from confusion to clarity, from being trapped to being set free! The Bible calls this transformation process "renewing your mind." When you were born again, your spirit was reborn, but your mind was not.

Renewing your mind is exactly what you'd expect—the process of retraining the way you think. Your mind is the result of all of your experiences—good and bad—up to this point. Your experiences have shaped a large part of who you are. However, you are more than what has happened to you; you are a child of God. God wonderfully crafted you, and He placed passions, gifts, talents, and a fulfilling purpose in you that He wants to accomplish—not *for* you but *through* you.

Renewing your mind is choosing to identify with who *God* says you are instead of what others have said, what your past says, or even what your present circumstances say about you.

You renew your mind by reading and meditating on the Scriptures—God's living message to you—and focusing on all that God has done for you and in you. Instead of flooding your eyes and ears with the corruption of this world, you immerse yourself in God's Word.

God is our Abba Father, and when you renew your mind, you adopt the way He sees you, accept the gifts that He has given you, and accomplish the things He said you can do! God created you and placed all your talents, passions, and dreams inside you. He knows exactly who you are and what you can do. It takes faith to hold on to what He says you are, what He says you have, and what He says you can do when your experiences tell you something entirely different.

That's why the process of renewing your mind is a daily one; you are constantly keeping a guard over what you watch and listen to, and, ultimately, what you think about. As we do this, day by day, we begin to transform into the happiest version of ourselves—the joyful, peaceful, and confident version that God always intended us to be. As we exchange our past for His promise, our dreams, passion, and purpose become more evident, and our love for God grows along with our desire to please Him.

Scriptures

Do not be conformed to this world (this age), fashioned after and adapted to its external, superficial customs, but be transformed (changed) by the entire renewal of your mind by its new ideals and its new attitude, so that you may prove for yourselves what is the good and acceptable and perfect will of God, even the thing which is good and acceptable and perfect in His sight for you.

–ROMANS 12:2 (AMPC)

Therefore if any man be in Christ, he is a new creature: old things are passed away; behold, all things are become new.

–2 CORINTHIANS 5:17 (KJV)

And he has taught you to let go of the lifestyle of the ancient man, the old self - life, which was corrupted by sinful and deceitful desires that spring from delusions. Now it's time to be made new by every revelation that's been given to you. And to be transformed as you embrace the glorious Christ-within as your new life and live in union with him! For God has re-created you all over again in his perfect righteousness, and you now belong to him in the realm of true holiness.

–EPHESIANS 4:22-24 (TPT)

Speak these words over your life:

I am being transformed daily. My thoughts, actions, and emotions are being shaped by the Word of God. I rely on the Lord for answers to the questions that arise in my life, and I refuse to depend on the wisdom of the world. I am growing in wisdom and stature as I absorb and act on the truth of God's Word. I will not be influenced by the problems, tests, or any crisis that comes my way. I will remain firmly planted and established in the integrity of God's Word. My perspective is becoming more godly day by day as I gain clarity and understanding as I apply the transforming principles found in God's Word. As my mind is being transformed, I am becoming more spiritually aware of God's plan and purpose for my life and increasing in my ability to believe and act according to His will for my life. I value and honor the gift of God's Word, and I will keep it in the highest place, as the final authority, in my life.

I Can Beat Addiction

This may shock you, but you were *created* to be *addicted*.

As we grow up in the natural, we should grow more and more *independent*. But as we grow up spiritually, we are to grow more and more *dependent*—on God. We develop a longing for His presence and rely more and more on His direction, peace, and joy.

God created us to be His kids and to live addicted to being with Him—His presence. He wanted us to always know the elation and satisfaction of living in a genuine relationship with our Heavenly Father. However, Satan has designed cheap "knock-offs" that try to serve as substitutes for living in close connection with God, and they are powerful weapons designed to steal your passion and dull your effectiveness.

Most know their addiction is harmful, whether it is drugs, alcohol, smoking, pornography, gambling, or a myriad of other things. Accepting its destructive nature is not the issue; we feel desperate and helpless when we try to overcome our addictions. You may have read every book you could find, prayed a thousand prayers, joined support groups, and done anything else you could think of. Or you may be in the midst of an internal war, living a double life where you feel more isolated with every relationship and every positive interaction, because they are complimenting or trying to connect with who you are *pretending* to be, and not the "real" you. Addictions always isolate, and eventually all who struggle with such things come to the same conclusion—"I can't beat this thing."

The truth is, that's exactly right. You alone cannot beat addiction, and you probably feel you aren't strong or disciplined enough to overcome.

But I have good news: *you are not alone*, and you never will be alone. God is with you, God is in you, God is for you, and He is on your side. With His help, you *will* overcome! The Bible says if you walk in the Spirit you will not gratify your fleshly desires. This means you can live your life united with Christ! It's not enough to quit the addiction; you must replace your dependency on it for a life of depending on *God*. He created you to be in an intimate relationship with Him, and nothing else will satisfy.

When you are at your weakest, God is at His strongest. When you need to escape, then escape into His presence. When you feel like giving in to your addiction, give into God instead. Utilize His wisdom and power found through the Bible and His Spirit. Bare your heart before Him, and use the mercy and power of His relationship to *beat addiction.*

Scriptures

The temptations in your life are no different from what others experience. And God is faithful. He will not allow the temptation to be more than you can stand. When you are tempted, he will show you a way out so that you can endure.

–1 CORINTHIANS 10:13 (NLT)

So submit to the authority of God. Resist the devil, stand firm against him and he will flee from you.

–JAMES 4:7 (AMP)

For we do not have a High Priest Who is unable to understand *and* sympathize *and* have a shared feeling with our weaknesses *and* infirmities *and* liability to the assaults of temptation, but One Who has been tempted in every respect as we are, yet without sinning. Let us then fearlessly *and* confidently *and* boldly draw near to the throne of grace (the throne of God's unmerited favor to us sinners), that we may receive mercy for our failures and find grace to help in good time for every need appropriate help and well-timed help, coming just when we need it.

–HEBREWS 4:15-16 (AMPC)

Speak these words over your life

I can do all things through Christ who strengthens me, and that includes beating addiction. Regardless of how I feel, how many times I have given into my addiction, or how long I've experienced failure in this area, I declare by faith I am free from this addiction. Though thoughts, feelings, and desires for the addiction may come, I will not give in because I am strong in the Lord and the power of His might. I am an overcomer, and addiction is just another thing that I overcome on my path to accomplishing my God-given destiny. My past is forgiven, my present is empowered by my union with Christ, and my future is bright with my promised destiny!

I Can Deal Wisely In My Affairs

The Bible says that wisdom is the principle thing, so go get it! God places getting wisdom as our top priority! When people hear the word "wisdom," often they picture an older individual with white hair sharing astonishing insight thanks to their many years of experience. Though there is truth in this picture, it can leave us with the connotation that wisdom can only be acquired through the passage of time. However, wisdom is not gained solely through personal experience or age but through an open heart and a listening ear. God even said,

"If any of you lacks wisdom, let him ask God, who gives generously to all without reproach, and it will be given him." James 1:5 (ESV)

Wisdom from our Father God is ready and available for us if we will just ask Him! This is one of the most underutilized gifts of Christianity; we think we are too busy and can't afford to take a break to read His Word and pray. The truth is, we can't afford *not* to! Sometimes the pressures of life force us into making rash, emotional, and irrational decisions instead of calm, well thought through decisions. It's wisdom to do your homework before deciding, to weigh the pro's and con's, and to seek the counsel of a trusted friend or a professional—but only *in addition to* and *not instead of* seeking guidance from God.

God poured His wisdom and insight into the Bible, yet too often we are praying for an answer from Heaven when we haven't spent the time to find out what He *already* told us to do in His Word. Read it, and learn from God's specific actions and the principles of His Word.

When it comes to a specific situation such as which school to attend, which career to pursue, who to marry, how to parent, what to buy, and where to invest, God will most often lead us through His peace. In Proverbs 3, it says all wisdom's ways are peace. God uses peace as our spiritual conscience or counselor. His Spirit guides us by it and lets us know what is safe and beneficial for us. When we feel that peace is missing, it shows us what is dangerous. So, pray and seek God, lean on His Spirit for help, and be sensitive to His peace in your life. Follow His wisdom, and you'll make good choices with wonderful outcomes.

Scriptures

But the wisdom that is from above is first pure, then peaceable, gentle, and easy to be intreated, full of mercy and good fruits, without partiality, and without hypocrisy.

–JAMES 3:17 (KJV)

If any of you lacks wisdom to guide him through a decision or circumstance, he is to ask of our benevolent God, who gives to everyone generously and without rebuke *or* blame, and it will be given to him.

–JAMES 1:5 (AMP)

My goal is that their hearts would be encouraged and united together in love so that they might have all the riches of assurance that come with understanding, so that they might have the knowledge of the secret plan of God, namely Christ. All the treasures of wisdom and knowledge are hidden in him.

–COLOSSIANS 2:2-3 (CEB)

11

Speak these words over your life

I know that God's Word guarantees that those who ask God for wisdom will be granted their request. So, I take this moment in time to pray: "Lord, I ask for wisdom concerning my affairs, and I thank you for direction, answers to questions, clarity, divine insights, supernatural ideas, and guidance in my day to day life to achieve the call you have placed upon my life. In the name of Jesus, Amen." Because God's wisdom is now operating in my life, I walk with divine clarity. I declare that I will be patient in distressing times, as I trust and lean on the Lord for His counsel and guidance with full assurance that His wisdom will come. I will not yield to anxiety when faced with difficult decisions; instead, I will lean on God and His wisdom on how to move forward.

I Can Do all Things Through Christ

You can do *all things* through *Christ* who strengthens you! Most Christians know this verse, but few have utilized the immeasurable power that is contained behind it. Most believers focus on the first part—"I can do all things" and when the going gets tough they forget the most important part— "through Christ who strengthens me." The Creator of every living thing is ready to infuse supernatural strength into your being—if you will only push past any doubt that your circumstances produce and rely on Him. Through Christ, you have the power to accomplish your purpose and strength to handle any storm that blows in your life. His strength, His joy, and His peace are *already yours*. But are you living that way?

We all face disappointments, challenges, and obstacles throughout our lives. Sometimes it is easier to switch into survival mode, where we are praying and believing God just to make it through the week or even the day. But God wants so much more than that for you! His desire is for you to get close to Him—so close that you tap into His strength and His stamina when yours begins to fail.

The closer you are to God and let Him into your life, the more He permeates it, filling every crack of weakness with His grace and strength. In Ephesians 6:10 (AMPC) it reads, *"In conclusion, be strong in the Lord **be empowered through your union with Him**; draw your strength from Him that strength which His boundless might provides."*

God wants us to lean on Him. He is our Father, and He did not design us to walk through life alone! He wants you to walk through life happy and fulfilled, completely void of fear, because you trust in Him completely. You are His child, and He wants to run this race of life together *with* you so that you cross the finish line together! When you talk to God in prayer, when you read His Word, and when you seek His will in your life, you are cultivating a relationship that transcends this life and will last all of eternity. You're planting seed in a relationship that will breathe purpose, strength, peace, and joy into your life now and forever. So don't doubt yourself for a second, because God doesn't. Instead, audaciously press forward in life with the spirit of a conqueror!

Scriptures

I can do all things which He has called me to do through Him who strengthens *and* empowers me to fulfill His purpose—I am self-sufficient in Christ's sufficiency; I am ready for anything and equal to anything through Him who infuses me with inner strength and confident peace.

–PHILIPPIANS 4:13 (AMP)

God can do anything, you know—far more than you could ever imagine or guess or request in your wildest dreams! He does it not by pushing us around but by working within us, his Spirit deeply and gently within us.

–EPHESIANS 3:20-21(MSG)

We pray that you may be strengthened *and* invigorated with all power, according to His glorious might, to attain every kind of endurance and patience with joy;

–COLOSSIANS 1:11 (AMP)

Speak these words over your life

I can do all things through Christ who strengthens *and* empowers me. I am self-sufficient in Christ's sufficiency; I am ready for anything and equal to anything through Him who infuses me with inner strength and confident peace. When I am weak in human strength, then am I truly strong, able, and powerful in divine strength. So, I will not falter on my convictions, and I will not let persecution cause me to draw back from the call of Christ upon my life, for I am strong in the Lord and in the power of His might. I will be successful in every endeavor because I am not alone; greater is He that is in me then he that is in the world.

I Can Live Confidently

Child of God, Ambassador of Christ, and Temple of the Holy Spirit—Jesus, through His redemption, separated you from your sin and bestowed these titles on you so that you can walk with unshakable confidence in a world of turmoil. Jesus said,

*"I have told you these things, so that in Me you may have perfect peace and **confidence**. In the world you have tribulation and trials and distress and frustration; but be of good cheer take courage; **be confident, certain, undaunted**! For I have overcome the world. I have deprived it of power to harm you and have conquered it for you." John 16:33 (AMPC)*

Many desire to be confident, to be bold, but they are afraid of failure and what may happen if they step out or stand up for their dreams and their God. You may have lost your confidence along the way due to your insecurities or failures, but if your confidence was based on your experiences, achievements, abilities or will power, it was doomed to be shattered from the start! As a Christian, true confidence is based on the God of the Bible and enters our lives through believing the words written by our Father God. It develops faith in us and a union with Christ that causes our confidence to soar. The Bible says Christ came to live in you and placed a new identity upon you. This means your confidence is due to an uncommon trust in who God says you are, what God says you have, and what God says you can do. There is no need to be afraid, insecure, or timid because you have Christ with you and His identity in you! You are able to approach life with the assurance that you have the God of Heaven's Armies as your ally!

Life is full of challenges, and more than likely we will make mistakes along the way, but as children of God, they should not cause us to lose our confidence. We have His strength to get up when life knocks us down, dust off our clothes, remind ourselves of who the Bible says we are and accept God's grace! Ultimate failure is not getting knocked down; it's staying down. But though you may fall seven times, you will rise again, confident in who God is and that He will work even this for your good.

Scriptures

I have told you these things, so that in Me you may have perfect peace *and* confidence. In the world you have tribulation *and* trials *and* distress *and* frustration; but be of good cheer take courage; be **confident**, certain, undaunted! For I have overcome the world. I have deprived it of power to harm you and have conquered it for you.

–JOHN 16:33 (AMPC)

Since we have such glorious hope (such joyful and **confident** expectation), we speak very freely *and* openly *and* fearlessly.

–2 CORINTHIANS 3:12 (AMPC)

Therefore my heart is glad and my glory my inner self rejoices; my body too shall rest *and* **confidently** dwell in safety,

–PSALMS 16:9 (AMPC)

Speak these words over your life

God has not given me a spirit of fear but power, love, and a sound mind. I am not timid or indecisive, and I do not fear what other people say or do. I do not fear what tomorrow holds or worry about how I will overcome the challenges of today, for the Greater One lives in me. I will not let criticisms and comments deter me from being bold. I declare that I am bold to speak my mind, to share my heart, and to profess my faith whenever it is necessary. God is the source of my confidence, and I am ready and willing for Him to speak His words through me whenever He requires it. I will not live out my days in quiet isolation; instead, I will live out my days with a confidence that cannot be stopped and a voice that cannot be silenced.

I Can Make a Difference

You do not need a stage, a crowd, or a mission field to make a difference. You don't need to have it all together, a million dollars in the bank, or a magnetic personality to make the world a better place.

Christians can underestimate the power of their influence. You come into contact with many people every day—clerks, servers, co-workers, friends, and of course your family. Each encounter you have with someone has the potential to have a positive impact on their life. To many people, you may be the only Bible that they will ever read and the only God they will ever see. There are people you can reach—acquaintances, friends, co-workers, family members—that the greatest preacher in the world will never reach. The Bible puts it like this:

"Don't begin by traveling to some far-off place to convert unbelievers. And don't try to be dramatic by tackling some public enemy. Go to the lost, confused people right here in the neighborhood." Matthew 10:5-6 (MSG)

Your encounter doesn't have to involve a grand gesture or sharing some profound truth. It's not preaching a sermon to everyone you talk to, either. A warm smile, a kind word, or a listening ear can make a powerful difference in someone's life. Whatever your small act of kindness may be, whether it's buying someone's meal or a cup of coffee or taking the time to simply ask how someone is doing and allowing yourself a few minutes to truly care about their answer, it is showing to them the love of God in a way that words can't. St. Augustine put it this way: "preach the gospel each and every day, and when necessary, use words."

However, when the situation calls for it, be bold with your faith. If you see someone in pain, ask if you can pray for them. Most people, even non-believers, will accept prayer if they are having a tough time. We have the cure for every suffering and the solution to every problem, and His name is Jesus! You can make a significant positive impact on those around you with a lot less effort than you think when you give God the opportunity to speak through you.

Scriptures

"Don't begin by traveling to some far-off place to convert unbelievers. And don't try to be dramatic by tackling some public enemy. Go to the lost, confused people right here in the neighborhood. Tell them that the kingdom is here. Bring health to the sick. Raise the dead. Touch the untouchables. Kick out the demons. You have been treated generously, so live generously."

–MATTHEW 10:5-8 (MSG)

Therefore, my beloved brethren, be firm (steadfast), immovable, always abounding in the work of the Lord always being superior, excelling, doing more than enough in the service of the Lord, knowing *and* being continually aware **that your labor in the Lord is not futile it is never wasted or to no purpose.**

–1 CORINTHIANS 15:58 (AMPC)

"Then these righteous ones will reply, 'Lord, when did we ever see you hungry and feed you? Or thirsty and give you something to drink? Or a stranger and show you hospitality? Or naked and give you clothing? When did we ever see you sick or in prison and visit you?' "And the King will say, **'I tell you the truth, when you did it to one of the least of these my brothers and sisters, you were doing it to me!'**

–MATTHEW 25:37-40 (NLT)

Speak these words over your life

I choose to make a difference in the lives of those that I come in contact with on a daily basis. I choose to let the love, light, and life of God shine through me today. I am sensitive to the needs of those around me, and I am determined to have a positive impact on their lives. I choose to be kind and considerate to my family, my friends, my co-workers, and everyone within my realm of influence. I refuse to ignore or be blind to the sufferings of those near me. I purpose in my heart to actively look for opportunities to inspire, influence, and impact the lives of those around me with Jesus' life-changing power.

I Can Fight

Life is a battle, and becoming a Christian equips you with the necessary weapons and armor to finally win instead of simply surviving. The Bible charges every believer to "Fight the good fight of faith." This is choosing to believe the promises of God above what anyone or any situation may convey to you. When this becomes your reality, then though the storms of life may rage and the waves of adversity may crash against you, you will remain solid as a rock, unmoved. You believe in a power greater than anything a storm could muster and a truth more sure than any foundation known to man: God and His Word!

So put your trust in God to see you through. Refuse to lay down and let the circumstances of life beat you down and rob you of your joy. Fight against the temptation to fear, worry, stress out, and doubt God's ability and willingness to take care of you. Courageously engage in combat with the various issues, imaginations, questions, and desires that arise in our minds by exposing them to the truth of God's Word and forcing them to conform to the Lordship of Jesus Christ. The Greater One is in you, Jesus is with you, God is *for* you, and you walk in the favor of God! The devil and all the powers of darkness are no match for you when you walk in that truth. You have the spirit of a conqueror in you—it's time to exercise it!

Read the Word of God, spend time in prayer, and speak His words aloud all day, but especially when you are tempted to doubt. Develop a spiritual resolve that won't crumble at the first sign of opposition. Develop a dogged determination to push through the obstacles and barriers that have been holding you back. Develop a spiritual fortitude that will carry you through any battle and on to victory.

Everything in this world seeks to pressure you and cause you to conform to its ideals and ways of living, but it is high time we as Christians start fighting back against the gross public display of debauchery and sin. So fight the good fight of faith with everything in you— fight against your own selfishness, against your own inadequacies, and against your weaknesses, knowing that when your strength begins to fail, God's strength will kick in!

Scriptures

Fight the good fight of the faith in the conflict with evil; take hold of the eternal life to which you were called, and for which you made the good confession of faith in the presence of many witnesses.

–1 TIMOTHY 6:12 (AMP)

For our struggle is not against flesh and blood contending only with physical opponents, but against the rulers, against the powers, against the world forces of this present darkness, against the spiritual *forces* of wickedness in the heavenly (supernatural) *places*.

–EPHESIANS 6:12 (AMP)

If your faith remains strong, even while surrounded by life's difficulties, you will continue to experience the untold blessings of God! True happiness comes as you pass the test with faith, and receive the victorious crown of life promised to every lover of God!

–JAMES 1:12 (TPT)

Speak these words over your life

I will fight the good fight of faith. I will not back down or be cowardly when faced with adverse circumstances. I will overcome the challenges and obstacles of this life with courage and confidence and the spirit of a conqueror. When the storms of life come, I will not allow myself to be overwhelmed by doubt and fear; instead, I will put my trust in God. God is on my side. I know that I am not fighting alone, and if God is for me then who can be against me? I will fight back against my own selfishness and weaknesses, and I will strive valiantly towards the purpose God has given me and to accomplish all that I have been tasked with.

I Can Enjoy Life

Life is meant to be an adventure we undertake, not an assignment we must endure! Jesus said that He came to the world so that we could have an *abundance of life*, with His peace navigating us through the dark places and His joy acting as our strength to push through the storm with a smile. Sadly, most are fighting to survive their lives instead of enjoying them. They believe the lie that their happiness—or lack thereof—is dependent upon their circumstances. If things are good, they are happy; if things are not good, then they are sad. This will cause them to be up one moment and down the next, happy one day and depressed the next. Our society has actually made it popular to be stressed, tired, and busy. This emotional rollercoaster lifestyle is a ride the world may ride, but believers can experience something different.

The truth is, we can choose to enjoy our life regardless of what we are experiencing.

It's not a matter of ignoring difficulties or faking happiness in the face of adversity. It's *choosing* happiness, it's *choosing* to base your joy, your security, and your peace on the solid foundation of the Word of God. It's choosing to remember all the benefits and blessings afforded to you as a child of God. It's choosing to cultivate a lifestyle of thanksgiving instead of complaining. It's resting in confident peace in the midst of trying times—because you have faith in your God!

There is no need to allow your circumstances to dictate your attitude or to let the pain of the past or the potential problems of the future rob you of the joy of today. It's time to enjoy your life, to live your life to the fullest with a spirit too close to God to be encumbered by negativity, doubt, and victim mentalities! Choose to smile right there in the middle of your messy life, walk on the bright side of the road, look up at the sky, trees, and birds, listen to fun music on the way to work or school, or watch something funny and laugh with the one you love. And when crisis strikes your life, like it does to all of us, stay full of joy and lean on God. Life was never meant to be endured but enjoyed.

Scriptures

You make known to me the path of life; in your presence there is fullness of joy; at your right hand are pleasures forevermore.

–PSALM 16:11 (ESV)

The thief comes only in order to steal and kill and destroy. I came that they may have *and* enjoy life, and have it in abundance to the full, till it overflows.

–JOHN 10:10 (AMP)

Enjoy the Lord, and he will give what your heart asks.

–PSALM 37:4 (CEB)

Rejoice in the Lord always delight, gladden yourselves in Him; again I say, Rejoice!

–PHILIPPIANS 4:4 (AMPC)

O taste and see that the Lord our God is good; how blessed fortunate, prosperous, and favored by God is the man who takes refuge in Him.

–PSALM 34:8 (AMP)

Speak these words over your life

I choose to be happy. I choose to base my joy, my security, and my peace on the solid foundation of the Word of God. This is the day that the Lord has made, and I will rejoice and make the choice to be glad in it! Even if this day presents adversity, challenges, and unwanted events, I will still choose to rejoice because I know that the Lord is with me. He encourages me, He supports me with His strong right arm, and He strengthens me. The joy of the Lord is my strength! I choose to cultivate a lifestyle of thanksgiving instead of complaining. I choose to trust that God has my back and to smile in the midst of trying times because I have faith in Him!

I will not allow my circumstances to dictate my attitude, and I will not allow the pain of the past or the potential problems of the future to rob me of the joy of today. I will enjoy my life. I will live my life to the fullest, because I am partaking of the abundant life Jesus came to give me. I reject negativity, doubt, and a victim mentality, and instead I choose joy!

I Can Forgive

Unforgiveness is a trap; it hinders our prayers, poisons our souls, and breeds bitterness. It casts shadows upon our otherwise happy lives. Your joy and peace begin to drain from your life. The sun doesn't shine as bright, flowers don't seem to hold the same beauty they once did, and the company you keep doesn't make you smile anymore when we do not forgive.

Unforgiveness is extremely toxic and wraps us up in bondage until we are controlled by our old memories instead of making any new ones. Many want to move on from the offense that was done to them or the mistakes that they made, yet the only way to truly move on is to forgive them or to forgive yourself. If you try to move on without forgiveness in your heart, then you will always be running away from your hurt, trying to create distance from your pain, but the problem is when we do not forgive, we have chosen to keep holding onto the poison that is killing us. However, the moment you choose to forgive those who have hurt you, you make the decision that allows

you to deal with your pain instead of running
from it. Now you can start living your life
pursuing your God-given destiny!

It may seem impossible, it may feel like
you'd be letting them win by forgiving, but
with God's help you can traverse the bumpy
terrain from a decision to true forgiveness. The
first step is to spend time with God. God loves
you, and when you spend time reading the
Bible, praying, and worshiping God, He is able
to pour His love into your heart. There is only
so much room in your heart, and the more love
He pours in, the more your shame and hatred
begin to flow out. The second step is to pour
out what God has poured in. You can't give
what you don't have; many fall short and hold
on to their bitterness and unforgiveness
because they haven't received forgiveness or
love on the level that they received hate and
shame. However, after receiving God's love
and forgiveness for you, you are able to replace
your bitterness with love and forgive the
unthinkable like God did for you. Then you get
to start the cycle of love all over again, filling
up on and pouring out God's love, instead of
the cycle of pain you once prescribed to.

Scriptures

If we freely admit that we have sinned and confess our sins, He is faithful and just (true to His own nature and promises) and will forgive our sins dismiss our lawlessness and continuously cleanse us from all unrighteousness everything not in conformity to His will in purpose, thought, and action.

−1 John 1:9 (AMPC)

But instead be kind and affectionate toward one another. Has God graciously forgiven you? Then graciously forgive one another in the depths of Christ's love.

−Ephesians 4:32 (TPT)

Judge not, and ye shall not be judged: condemn not, and ye shall not be condemned: forgive, and ye shall be forgiven:

−Luke 6:37 (KJV)

Be gentle and forbearing with one another and, if one has a difference (a grievance or complaint) against another, readily pardoning each other; even as the Lord has freely forgiven you, so must you also forgive.

−Colossians 3:13 (AMPC)

Speak these words over your life

I am thankful that I have been forgiven. God, in His mercy and by His grace, has forgiven me of all my sins, mistakes, and shortcomings. I choose to accept God's forgiveness and His unconditional love. Even though I may not feel it, by faith I know that according to God's Word, I am righteous, in right standing with God, and He sees me as someone who has never sinned. It is by this state of righteousness bought by God's unconditional love through the shed blood of Jesus Christ that I am able to echo that same spirit of forgiveness and love to those around me. So, with the Lord's help and by the power of the Holy Spirit, I choose to wholly and completely forgive all of those who have hurt me, betrayed me, defamed my character, ignored me, or caused emotional or physical damage to me. By faith, I choose to let go of every one of those grudges and walk in the freedom that God paid for me.

I Can Rest

Life can get very tiresome—and not just physically. Trying to be the perfect spouse, parent, or employee causes a lot of mental and emotional wear and tear. We experience the pressure to conform to the expectations of others, to be a good friend, model citizen, dutiful churchgoer, or tireless volunteer—the list could go on and on. Each one of these things has the potential to produce worry, anxiety, and stress in our lives. As the years go on, as a society we keep looking in all the wrong places to get the rest we so desperately need. Our lives are getting busier and busier, but more caffeine and less sleep are not the solutions—nor are stress relieving scents, lotions, and oils the best way to cope. Obviously, being sleep deprived affects our performance and takes its toll on our health, but there is a greater threat that has crept into our society: a weariness of the soul. And this is the kind of tired you can't sleep off.

Walking through life when you are weary will cause you to go down a destructive path where you begin to hate what you once loved, and ultimately you will adopt a selfish and self-destructive behavior. Many of us settle just for a moment of "peace"—time away from it all—but the problem with this kind of momentary cease-fire is we come back to the same life we tried to escape.

Real rest comes from the Lord. He said it Himself in Matthew 11:28-30 (MSG): *"Are you tired? Worn out? Burned out on religion?* **Come to me. Get away with me and you'll recover your life. I'll show you how to take a real rest.** *Walk with me and work with me— watch how I do it. Learn the unforced rhythms of grace. I won't lay anything heavy or ill-fitting on you.* **Keep company with me and you'll learn to live freely and lightly."**

You see, the rest we are all seeking can only be found in Christ. Resting in the Lord is casting all the cares of your life on God— giving Him your troubles, your anxieties, your insecurities, your worries, and all your stress. Though, it's not enough to just cast the cares; it's up to us to leave those cares with Him by placing our complete confidence and trust in Him. Then we will be able to take a real rest, knowing we are in safe hands.

Scriptures

Come to Me, all you who labor and are heavy-laden *and* overburdened, and I will cause you to rest. I will ease and relieve and refresh your souls.

–MATTHEW 11:28 (AMPC)

But they that wait upon the Lord shall renew their strength; they shall mount up with wings as eagles; they shall run, and not be weary; and they shall walk, and not faint.

–ISAIAH 40:31 (KJV)

Casting the whole of your care all your anxieties, all your worries, all your concerns, once and for all on Him, for He cares for you affectionately *and* cares about you watchfully.

–1 PETER 5:7 (AMPC)

And he said, My presence shall go with thee, and I will give thee rest.

–EXODUS 33:14 (KJV)

The LORD is my shepherd. I lack nothing. He lets me rest in grassy meadows; he leads me to restful waters;

–PSALM 23:1-2 (CEB)

When you lie down, you shall not be afraid; yes, you shall lie down, and your sleep shall be sweet.

–PROVERBS 3:24 AMPC)

Speak these words over your life

Before He left this earth, Jesus said that He gave us His peace. He called it, "a peace that passes human understanding." By faith, I choose to receive that peace and step into the rest He offers me. I cast all my cares, worries, frustrations, and anxieties on Him. Even in the midst of the challenges, disappointments, and unexpected setbacks, even in the worst situations that life can offer, I make the choice here and now, I choose—and will always choose—to trust in God. According to His Word, I qualify to receive a supernatural rest that is only reserved for those who put their trust in the Lord. By faith, I take that rest. I know that the Lord will act as my refuge forever, sheltering me from the storm, providing a place of peace and an opportunity for rest with the promise that He will never leave me and will always be with me.

I Can Be Intimate With God

God loves you. You are His child, and He loves you unconditionally. He desires to spend time with you. Most people's concept of Christianity is that it is a religion with a long list of rules that they must obey in order to escape hell. It inaccurately paints God as an authoritarian tyrant and falsely describes the Christian life in terms of condemnation, fear, and penitence. They think it demands serving God out of duty and that your acceptance is based on your piety, holiness, and good deeds. However, this type of religious lifestyle makes for a fickle Christian walk, because it bases your sense of self-worth on what you do instead of what God has already done for you.

This is not the Christianity that Jesus died for us to gain!

Have you ever wondered why God created us? It was because He wanted children of His own! He even made us in His own image! So, when Adam and Eve messed up and cut humanity off from a relationship with God, God stopped at nothing to restore fellowship with His beloved children. He even gave up His son,

Jesus, as a substitute for our sin to accomplish this goal. That's how much He desired to have a relationship with us. He was willing to watch His boy tortured and killed to give us the chance to run into His open arms. This is true Christianity—relationship. In a relationship, we serve out of love and loyalty, not fear and duty.

Like any relationship, developing this intimacy doesn't happen overnight; it takes time. The easiest way to start down the path of growing more intimate with God is simply by spending more time with Him. He said He would never leave you or forsake you, which means you can talk to Him as much as you want. You can read the Bible, gaining insight into the way God thinks, as well as hearing what pleases and displeases your Father. God will be as much a part—or as little of a part—of your life as you want Him to be. As you value His words, get to know Him, develop your faith in Him, and spend time talking to Him throughout your days, regardless of your circumstances. Then your relationship will grow, and an intimacy between you that is unique and special to both of you will develop. This is what Christianity is about—an intimate relationship with your Father God.

Yes, furthermore, I count everything as loss compared to the possession of the priceless privilege (the overwhelming preciousness, the surpassing worth, and supreme advantage) of knowing Christ Jesus my Lord *and* of progressively becoming more deeply *and* intimately acquainted with Him of perceiving and recognizing and understanding Him more fully and clearly. For His sake I have lost everything and consider it all to be mere rubbish (refuse, dregs), in order that I may win (gain) Christ (the Anointed One).

–PHILIPPIANS 3:8 (AMPC)

In conclusion, be strong in the Lord **be empowered through your union with Him;** draw your strength from Him that strength which His boundless might provides.

–EPHESIANS 6:10 (AMPC)

"Have I not commanded you? Be strong and courageous! Do not be terrified or dismayed (intimidated), **for the LORD your God is with you wherever you go.**"

–JOSHUA 1:9 (AMP)

'Do not fear anything, for I am with you; Do not be afraid, for I am your God. I will strengthen you, be assured I will help you; I will certainly take hold of you with My righteous right hand a hand of justice, of power, of victory, of salvation.'

–ISAIAH 41:10 (AMP)

Speak these words over your life

Today marks a new day in my relationship with God. I make the choice to prioritize God above everything else in my life. When I grow tired and weary, I will run to Him for rest. When I become stressed, worried, anxious, or afraid, I will cast my care upon Him, for I know how deeply He cares for me. I choose to keep God in the center of my life and in the forefront of my mind. My actions are out of a heart to please Him, and I will put to death my selfish and carnal nature daily. I choose to feed on God's Word, to spend time with Him in prayer, and go to Him first when I need help, instead of the last resort. I purpose in my heart to grow closer and more intimate with my Heavenly Father.

I Can Make It Through

No matter what you are going through, there are two things that are essential for you to remember: The first is that Jesus said that He would never leave you or forsake you. The second is that through faith in God—both in His Word and in His Spirit—you have the power, strength, fortitude, and resources to make it through any challenge, crisis, or difficulty you face. Sure, this life has difficulties and challenges, but we are never helpless, without support, or powerless. We can sail through the storms of life with an undaunted spirit. Jesus Himself said,

"I have told you these things, so that in Me you may have perfect peace and confidence. In the world you have tribulation and trials and distress and frustration; but be of good cheer take courage; be confident, certain, undaunted! For I have overcome the world. I have deprived it of power to harm you and have conquered it for you." John 16:33 (AMPC)

God knew you would experience problems; the fact that problems are in your life are

not indicative of your shortcomings or a lack
of faithfulness; nor are they a result of judg-
ment on God's part. We live in a world in
chaos, and problems come because of it. So,
quit focusing on how or why the issue is in
your life and start focusing on the solution to
your problem: Jesus.

You see, the only way any situation can get
the better of you is if you give it permission.
Your peace, joy, attitude, faith, hope, character,
and love are based on God, His Word, and His
faithfulness, which are eternally stable and
trustworthy. So no matter what situation comes
your way—whether you messed up, it was an
accident, or it was an attack—the bottom line is
that God has provided the grace, strength, and
guidance to make it through—and to be victorious! Sometimes it's easy to be overwhelmed
when in the middle of a crisis—to let our
emotions override our faith and dwell on the
issue as if it wasn't already taken care of. But
remember what Jesus said: you are not alone!
Refocus your attention back on God instead of
your problem by speaking His words, and your
emotions will follow suit. You can and will
make it through!

Scriptures

I've said these things to you so that you will have peace in me. In the world you have distress. But be encouraged! I have conquered the world."

–JOHN 16:33 (CEB)

Is anyone crying for help? GOD is listening, ready to rescue you. If your heart is broken, you'll find GOD right there; if you're kicked in the gut, he'll help you catch your breath. Disciples so often get into trouble; still, GOD is there every time.

–PSALMS 34:17-19 (MSG)

When I was desperate, I called out, and GOD got me out of a tight spot.

–PSALMS 34:6 (MSG)

Speak these words over your life

No matter what I am facing today, with the Lord's help, I can make it through. By the power of the Holy Spirit and the truth of God's Word, I will overcome. He sustains me, encourages me, strengthens me, and empowers me to overcome. Even if I get hedged in, pressed on every side, troubled, and oppressed in every way, I will not be crushed because greater is He that is in me than anyone else who could come against me. Even if I suffer embarrassments and am perplexed and feel unable to find a way out, I will not give in to despair because I know Jesus *always* makes a way out! Even if I am pursued, persecuted, and hard driven, I refuse to worry or be afraid because the Lord is with me, and He is always with me, upholding me. Even if I am knocked off my feet and struck down to the ground, I am not knocked out of the fight because my God is the God of hope, and as long as I don't give up and I cling to that everlasting hope that Christ provides, I cannot be destroyed.

I Can Speak Life

God spoke, and the world came into exis-
tence. He made us in His image, and our words
are much more significant than many people
have been led to believe. The Bible even says,

*"Death and life are in the power of the
tongue, and they who indulge in it shall eat the
fruit of it for death or life." Proverbs 18:21
(AMPC)*

Our words hold the power of life and death,
and yet so many times, we let our mouth run
wild instead of controlling the words that come
out of it. Our words should not convey negativity and harsh criticism but rather minister life
and hope to those who hear them. Many have
believed the lie, "Live how you feel, say what
you want." It sounds good, but its true decep-
tion lies in the fact that it only caters to one
person: you. Following this philosophy will
lead you down a road that eventually creates a
self-centered critic that breeds negativity in
your life and in the lives of those around you.

You shouldn't express every feeling or
thought that comes to your mind; instead, you

should examine your thoughts and filter them so that your words, even if they must convey constructive criticism or a harsh truth, will still leave the hearer uplifted, instead of downtrodden. The world is full of critics, but it is desperate for some encouragers! The Bible tells us that our words govern our direction in life. This means you have the capacity to change your situation regardless of what it may be! You never have to be a victim. You may have made mistakes that have put you in a bad spot. Though the world may have abused you in any number of ways, it's through God's Word that you can find forgiveness and healing, and confessing His Word with your mouth releases the life-shaping power that resides within your spirit. The Bible says God's Word is life! If you want to speak life over any situation, then find out what *God* has to say about it, and then speak it out loud with faith. Our mouths and minds should be filled with God's words, because then they will be filled with life. Speak God's Word over your life and with those you come in contact with. Speak life!

Scriptures

We are destroying sophisticated arguments and every exalted *and* proud thing that sets itself up against the true knowledge of God, **and *we are* taking every thought *and* purpose captive to the obedience of Christ,**

–2 Corinthians 10:5 (AMP)

A bit in the mouth of a horse controls the whole horse. A small rudder on a huge ship in the hands of a skilled captain sets a course in the face of the strongest winds. A word out of your mouth may seem of no account, but it can accomplish nearly anything—or destroy it!

–James 3:3-5 (MSG)

By faith that is, with an inherent trust and enduring confidence in the power, wisdom and goodness of God we understand that the worlds (universe, ages) were framed *and* created formed, put in order, and equipped for their intended purpose **by the word of God**, so that what is seen was not made out of things which are visible.

–Hebrews 11:3 (AMP)

Speak these words over your life

I speak life, health, healing, strength, and vitality to my body. I command my body to operate and function the way God intended it to. I speak peace, joy, supernatural intelligence, and understanding to my mind. I command my mind to be quick, sharp, witty, strong, at peace, full of joy, and alert. I have the mind of Christ and a body that will not hold me back from what God has called me to accomplish on this earth. I speak over my finances, and I declare that my debts are being reduced and eliminated. I claim the inheritance of abundance that He's given to me as His child. I have enough to accomplish all that I am called to do, with plenty left over for me to give and enjoy. I speak over every one of my relationships, and I declare that they be fruitful, that all bitterness and negativity must go, and to make way for love and peace. I call my family healthy, safe, and blessed. Finally, I declare that I will accomplish the purpose God has given me, I will be sensitive to the leading of the Holy Spirit, and I will enjoy a life full of all that God has given me.

I Can Be Led By The Holy Spirit

You can follow the Spirit of God. The Holy Spirit came to live and dwell in you when you accepted Jesus as your personal Lord and Savior. Many have been taught that the Holy Spirit is some fantastical being that is unpredictable and mysterious. However, the Bible clearly identifies who the Holy Spirit is and what He is here to do. He is our Helper, Counselor, and Teacher. He helps us understand the Scriptures and ultimately assists us in fulfilling God's plan for our lives, helping us navigate the tumultuous waters of life.

Though there are many ways He can lead us, there are two ways that He leads that are most common in our everyday life: through the Bible and through peace. The Holy Spirit always confirms the Bible, He will never contradict it. If you have a question of what to do, the first place you should always check is the Bible. The more you read the Word, the more you will be able to recognize the difference between your own thoughts and ideas and the promptings of the Holy Spirit. The Bible is inspired by the Holy Spirit and conveys God's thoughts to us. The more you listen to and read the way God thinks, the more you are able to recognize and then act on the thoughts and leadings He gives to you through His Spirit.

The second way He leads is by His peace. Pressures and worries come at us daily, but when we place our confident trust in God to help us, then He replaces our burdens with His peace. The Bible calls it "a peace that passes human understanding," and that is because it is a level of peace that doesn't make natural sense when you have problems all around you. It's through this state of being known as peace that we are able to discern where to go and what to do. Before making a decision, check your heart and see if you feel peace about doing it or if you feel an absence of peace concerning it. So, ask for the Holy Spirit's help, seek His counsel, fill up on the Bible, follow after His peace, and you'll find yourself right where you need to be—following the Holy Spirit.

Scriptures

For all who are led by the Spirit of God are children of God.

–Romans 8:14 (NLT)

And let the peace (soul harmony which comes) from Christ rule (act as umpire continually) in your hearts deciding and settling with finality all questions that arise in your minds, in that peaceful state to which as members of Christ's one body you were also called to live. And be thankful (appreciative), giving praise to God always.

–Colossians 3:15 (AMPC)

…What eye has not seen and ear has not heard and has not entered into the heart of man, all that God has prepared (made and keeps ready) for those who love Him who hold Him in affectionate reverence, promptly obeying Him and gratefully recognizing the benefits He has bestowed. Yet to us God has unveiled *and* revealed them by *and* through His Spirit, for the Holy Spirit searches diligently, exploring *and* examining everything, even sounding the profound and bottomless things of God the divine counsels and things hidden and beyond man's scrutiny.

–1 Corinthians 2:9(b)-10 (AMPC)

Speak these words over your life

The Holy Spirit is with me. I choose to lean on Him as my teacher, my guide, and also as a very dear friend. I shall trust Him, and look to Him, to reveal the truth in God's Word, and the specific nature of God's plan and purpose for my life. I endeavor to grow closer and be more sensitive to the voice of the Holy Spirit so that He may lead, guide, and direct me in all things. With His help, I will be able to change and transform daily through the application of divine truths, insights, and revelations, and through the impartation of the Holy Spirit. In times of trouble, I choose to trust in God, and His Holy Spirit to warn me and guide me out. And finally, I choose to let the Holy Spirit shine through me producing goodness and mercy in my wake.

I Can Achieve My Dreams

Your life today is mostly the product of the decisions you have made in the past. This can be a sad reality for some who feel like failures, with their dreams unrealized and their goals unfulfilled. And if their story was to end today, it would be a tragedy indeed. But the good news is that this is not the end of your story. You are still writing your story with every decision you make. While you draw breath, there is hope for you and hope for your dreams.

Do not be discouraged if your life has not turned out the way that you thought, because just like your past has determined your present, your present determines your future! It's time to dream again! Change your future with the decisions you make—starting today! In the past, you may have tried to make it on your own merits and abilities, but now it's time to lean on God for support and guidance. It will take discipline—your dream won't just fall in your lap—but you have your Father God as a companion and the Holy Spirit as your guide to fulfill your destiny. The truth is, you are not the only one dreaming. You are God's kid, He has a dream for you too—to see you fulfilled, successful, with a wonderful family, and most importantly an intimate relationship with Himself.

God has a place where you will flourish, a job that He has grace for you to do, a family for you to cherish, and ultimately a disposition of joyful peace in all of your endeavors. It's not a fantasy; it's your reality! God never intended you to go into any venture or to undertake anything alone. Whatever it is, God wants to be a part of it, and He wants to help you in every area of your life. It doesn't matter how old you are or how many times you have failed, God is ready to help you achieve your goals and give shape to the dreams He's placed inside of you! Don't spend time dwelling on the impossibilities of what it will take; spend time meditating on how big and how good your Father God is! As you pray and seek God for your future, your first step towards your destiny is simple—love God and love others! As you keep these two directives as your guidelines for the decisions you make, you'll be on the right path towards your—and God's—dream for your life.

Scriptures

For with God nothing shall be impossible.
—LUKE 1:37 (KJV)

"For I know the plans I have for you," says the Lord. "They are plans for good and not for disaster, to give you a future and a hope."
—JEREMIAH 29:11 (NLT)

Roll your works upon the Lord commit and trust them wholly to Him; He will cause your thoughts to become agreeable to His will, and so shall your plans be established and succeed.
—PROVERBS 16:3 (AMPC)

For you have need of steadfast patience and endurance, so that you may perform and fully accomplish the will of God, and thus receive and carry away and enjoy to the full what is promised.
—HEBREWS 10:36 (AMPC)

Speak these words over your life

I declare that I will fulfill my God-given destiny. I will achieve the dreams and the goals that the Lord has given me. Even if I have been sidetracked or distracted, even if the mistakes and failures of my past have threatened to derail my future, even if I feel battered, beaten, and bruised with everything in me begging to throw in the towel and give up, even then, I will not concede defeat. These dreams I have are not just mine; they were placed inside me by God, and with His help, I will fight with all that I am to see those goals accomplished and dreams realized. And when my strength fades, I know I haven't even scratched the surface of the wealth and depth of God's immeasurable power He made available to me, His child. So, I boldly declare I can, and I *will*, achieve my dreams!

I Can Rise

The same Spirit that raised Christ from the dead lives in you! It doesn't matter how deep or how dark your pit may be; you do not have to be buried by your failures. Your shame and regret do not have to remain as a tomb for your ambitions, and your spirit does not have to be broken. That same unbreakable Spirit that ripped Christ out of the clutches of death and sin, causing Him to ascend on high, can also raise you out of whatever pit you find yourself in!

The time has come for you to RISE! *Rise* out of your bed of affliction. *Rise* out of depression and despair. *Rise* above the opinions of others. *Rise* out of the shame and regret of your failures. *Rise* out of mediocrity. *Rise* out of the sin that has ensnared you. It's time to base your identity on who *Christ* says you are instead of your past. It's time to throw off the weights that once held you, allow hope to rise within your heart, dare to dream, dare to discover, dare to overcome, dare to keep trying, and dare to act upon what you believe!

You are a child of God, empowered and equipped with the mightiest weapon of all, faith in God! Your past cannot hold you any longer! Your *future* is bright because your *present* is filled with Christ! He was the first one to rise, and He's paved the way for each and every one of us to rise just as He did. God sent Jesus to pave the way, to give hope, and to restore His children to their rightful place as heirs to His kingdom.

The darkness can be familiar and seem inescapable, but you were made by and for the light. Don't allow your circumstances to shake you from believing the truth of God's Word. Even when the storm winds blow, hold fast to the words He has spoken to you and rise out of the pit by acting upon them! Jesus is your companion, your friend, your advocate, your help, and your support! If you slip, He'll catch you every time. If you get lost, He'll find you. If your strength fails, He'll carry you until you catch your breath. There is hope for you! There is freedom and joy in your future.

I CAN RISE

Scriptures

Arise from the depression and prostration in which circumstances have kept you—rise to a new life! Shine (be radiant with the glory of the Lord), for your light has come, and the glory of the Lord has risen upon you!

–ISAIAH 60:1 (AMPC)

for the light makes everything visible. This is why it is said, "Awake, O sleeper, **rise up** from the dead, and Christ will give you light."

–EPHESIANS 5:14 (NLT)

Yes, God raised Jesus to life! And since God's Spirit of Resurrection lives in you, he will also raise your dying body to life by the same Spirit that breathes life into you!

–ROMANS 8:11 (TPT)

Speak these words over your life

The same Spirit that raised Christ Jesus from the dead lives in me. That resurrection power gives me the strength, fortitude, and power to rise above anything that would try to hold me down and keep me from living life to the fullest measure. I dare to overcome. I dare to keep trying. I dare to act upon what I believe!

I will rise!

I will rise out of depression and despair. I will *rise* out of shame and regret. I will *rise* out of mediocrity. I will *rise* out of sin. I will *rise* above the opinions of others. I choose to base my identity on who Christ says I am. I'm throwing off the weights that once held me. I dare to dream. I dare to discover. I am a child of God, empowered and equipped with the mightiest weapon of all, faith in God! My past cannot hold me any longer! My future is bright because my present is filled with Christ!

About the Authors

Keith Provance, involved in Christian publishing for more than 40 years, is the founder and president of Word and Spirit Publishing, a company dedicated to the publishing and world-wide distribution of scriptural, life-changing books. He also works as a publishing consultant to national and international ministries. Keith continues to write with his wife and with his son Jake. He and his wife, Megan, have authored a number of bestselling books with total sales of over 2 million copies. They reside in Tulsa, Oklahoma and are the parents of three sons, Ryan, Garrett, and Jake.

You may contact Keith at
Keith@WordAndSpiritPublishing.com

Jake Provance is a successful young writer, who has written seven books and has plans to write several more. Jake's first book, Keep Calm & Trust God, has sold more than 500,000 copies. Jake is a graduate of Domata Bible School in Tulsa, OK, and has a call on his life to work in pastoral care ministry, with a particular passion to minister to young adults. Jake and his wife, Leah, live in Tulsa, OK.

Check out Jake's blog at Life-Speak.com

You may contact Jake at
Jake@WordAndSpiritPublishing.com

Other inspirational books
by Jake & Keith Provance

Keep Calm & Trust God - Volume 1

Keep Calm & Trust God - Volume 2

Keep Calm
(hardback gift edition - includes volumes 1&2)

Let Not Your Heart be Troubled

Scriptural Prayers for Victorious Living

I Am What the Bible Says I Am

I Have What the Bible Says I Have

I Can Do What the Bibles Says I Can Do

I AM

WHAT THE BIBLE SAYS I AM

JAKE & KEITH PROVANCE

I AM WHAT THE BIBLE SAYS I AM

Who are you . . . *really?*

For many people, answering that question is a daily struggle. It often seems as though our identity is in a constant state of flux—based on what we allow to define us. Whether it is the type of childhood we had, our relationships, experiences, social status, occupation, or social environment—all of these aspects of our identity can contribute to the way we view ourselves.

The Bible tells us that once we become a Christian, we become a new person with a brand-new identity from God. An identity based on a spiritual transformation. An identity based on how God sees us, not on our own opinions or the opinions of others.

The truths in this book will help you reshape and redefine your identity based on God's Word. It will reveal who you really are and how you can live a life full of joy, confidence, and surety. *I Am . . .* is about who *you are*. It is the perfect tool to discover the reality of who you are in Christ and walk in the fullness of the inheritance He has provided for you.

I HAVE

WHAT THE BIBLE SAYS I HAVE

JAKE & KEITH PROVANCE

I HAVE WHAT THE BIBLE SAYS I HAVE

Many walk through this life unaware of the wealth of God's gifts that they have been given to enjoy.

They walk distressed, worried, and afraid when God has provided them peace, joy, and hope. They spend their lives at the mercy of their circumstances when God has given them the grace and the faith to handle any situation.

God has given us everything we will ever need to face any challenge that may come our way. The best part about God's gifts is that they are unmerited. This means you don't have to sacrifice anything to obtain them, you don't have to live a perfect life to earn them, and you don't have to work hard to be worthy of them. All of His gifts are already yours, so all you have to do is accept them.

God lays out every detail of His amazing gifts in His Word, the Bible. Whether you are a new believer, or you have been one of God's kids for a while, the purpose of this little book is to help you see the gifts and promises found in His Word and empower you to live the life for which God destined you to live.